A Quality Life

A Quality Life

A Person Profoundly Affected by Multiple Disabilties:
A Life Profoundly Affected by and Affecting
Those Who Come in Contact with Him

Christine T. Seiler, PhD

BALBOA.
PRESS
A DIVISION OF HAY HOUSE

ISBN: 978-1-4525-5305-4 (sc)
ISBN: 978-1-4525-5304-7 (e)

Library of Congress Control Number: 2012910627

Balboa Press books may be ordered through booksellers or by contacting:

Balboa Press
A Division of Hay House
1663 Liberty Drive
Bloomington, IN 47403
www.balboapress.com
1-(877) 407-4847

Because of the dynamic nature of the Internet, any web addresses or links contained in this book may have changed since publication and may no longer be valid. The views expressed in this work are solely those of the author and do not necessarily reflect the views of the publisher, and the publisher hereby disclaims any responsibility for them.

The author of this book does not dispense medical advice or prescribe the use of any technique as a form of treatment for physical, emotional, or medical problems without the advice of a physician, either directly or indirectly. The intent of the author is only to offer information of a general nature to help you in your quest for emotional and spiritual well-being. In the event you use any of the information in this book for yourself, which is your constitutional right, the author and the publisher assume no responsibility for your actions.

Any people depicted in stock imagery provided by Thinkstock are models, and such images are being used for illustrative purposes only.
Certain stock imagery © Thinkstock.

Printed in the United States of America

Balboa Press rev. date: 7/5/2012

For Nancy

Mom and sister

with love and admiration

Contents

Preface

This is a collection of stories that were written through the years in moments of inspiration with the intention of trying to capture in writing how profoundly I had been affected by my nephew Cory as—together—we have participated in life.

These stories have been kept in a three ring binder with a picture of Cory on the cover and the following title:

A Quality Life
A Person Profoundly Affected by Multiple
Disabilities: A Life Profoundly Affected by and
Affecting Those Who Come in Contact with Him.

A Collaborative Work including Short Stories
by Cory Seiler as told by his Aunt Chris and by Christine T.
Seiler, Ph.D.

This title still, although clumsy, captures my intentions well.

For clarity, a story that has been written from Cory's perspective as I imagined it to be will include in its title "by Cory Seiler as told by his Aunt Chris". A story written from my perspective will include in its title "by Aunt Chris".

Names, except for immediate family, have been changed. But, it is my hope that these stories do justice in honoring each person's contribution to Cory's quality of life. Those from the past are remembered with great fondness. Those from the present continue to be appreciated for their presence in our lives.

As Cory has a circle of supports to assist him in living his life I have had a circle of supports in completing this project.

I would like to thank my sister and Cory's mom, Nancy. Without her there would be no stories to tell. She has provided inspiration, a parent perspective, help with recollecting, as well as technical assistance. Her input gave me the confidence to take this collection of stories to the next level: publication.

I would like to thank the team at Balboa Press for their encouragement in getting things started and their guidance throughout the publishing process.

Finally, I would like to thank German Armijo for his unending belief in me and that I had a book that needed to be published.

To Moms, Dads, and Family Members:

I hope that you will be both informed by the struggles and energized by the successes within these stories. I hope that you find recognition for the contributions you have made in supporting your own son or daughter or family member. I want to thank you for being the support that enables your son or daughter or family member to make his or her contribution to my world. I have no doubt that your efforts make our world a better place.

In Profound Appreciation

by Aunt Chris

Cory and Aunt Chris

"Profoundly affected by multiple disabilities" this is the way we have come to describe my nephew, Cory, in situations where describing his level of disability is helpful. I remember being told that they no longer use the label "profound," but now group these individuals within the "severe" category. I remember noticing that the textbooks that were about teaching those with severe disabilities didn't include pictures of kids like Cory. Kids with severe disabilities would seem to be "higher functioning." What I soon began to appreciate was that the label "profound" more accurately describes our profound inability to have a clue what abilities are present in an individual at this "level of disability." I wonder if it wouldn't be of more value to keep a label that reminds us that for these individuals we are more likely to see so much less when there is so much more. What I do know is that I profoundly appreciate what Cory has brought into my life.

Our lack of ability to see these individuals for who they really are was underlined for me on July 17, 1993 when we brought Cory into the hospital. The doctors had not started to explore what was wrong with Cory. They hadn't determined that he was dying. So, I couldn't understand why the doctor asked my sister, "Do we resuscitate?" Was it because the doctor just didn't appreciate Cory's quality of life? I wrote this letter to Cory that night. I read it to him the next day feeling that in some way he would understand me.

Dear Cory,

Thank you, Cory, for including me as one of those who gets to share "the look" with you when you want to let them know you care. You know the one I am talking about. The one where you lean forward placing your forehead against mine and stare up into my eyes with that ridiculously huge grin—which is actually an imitation of your mother's ridiculously huge grin.

Thank you for conversing with me about your favorite things such as lights "looh a a lih", planes "whaz ah?", and whether I need a sweater "cloz on?" Oh, and bridges and motorcycles too.

Thank you for sharing your routine with me the last time I went with you wheeling at the mall. I would have never noticed the mirrors on the steps without you pointing them out to me. As the old routine goes: "looh a ah", "whoz ah i ehr?", "Is that Cory in there?", "Cory i ehr". I guess I have to also thank you for harassing me about my fear of heights by wheeling next to the edge on the second floor. It shows me you know me well and love me—harassment being a Seiler way of showing love. (By the way, I checked with your mother. She says you don't do that with her so you have no excuses. Just like my reaction, huh?)

Thank you for putting up with my doing everything backwards when I take care of you. You know I love you (I tell you so, hoping you'll be understanding), so you accept my shortcomings. I know you're thinking, "That poor Aunt Chris. She doesn't know what she's doing."

Thank you for telling me I'm wonderful: "Wuu-underr!" when I finally get something right.

Thank you for always being there when I am down. I remember when I was just a teenager and you were three or four. I was upset (probably about a boyfriend) so I went to cuddle with you. You pulled me out of myself. You reminded me that there are more important things in life. There was love, and you loved me. I remember your first sentence: "I yu ooo…" I love you, Cory. I am 32 now and you are 20. I can still count on you for a cuddle.

Thank you for showing me that there are people out there—especially kids—that are capable of looking beyond a person's disabilities to the person. Really, it is okay that your classmates ignore me when they say hi to you at the mall or when one cashes us out at the grocery store (being of the older generation I guess that is to be expected).

I believe that your being a student in regular education classes in your neighborhood high school, and being employed by the same employers as the rest of us, and exercising at the mall like other exercisers in the community has had a significant positive impact. Thank you for contributing to making my world a better place. (But I've often wondered, since you work at the same place I rent videos, couldn't you get me a discount or something?)

Thank you, Cory, for helping me to recognize that my notions of humanness and quality of life have been limited by my position of so called privilege. Without you I would have always measured quality of life by abilities and advantages. On one side of the fence the grass would have always been greener and on the other side of the fence—weeds. Never would I have been in my own yard enjoying the grass under my bare feet if I hadn't had you to set an example. I have always sensed a wisdom in your silence. You take life as it comes—recognizing the wonder in things I take for granted while taking in stride things I consider unthinkable.

I have watched you respond to those who reach out to you and ignore those who haven't come to realize what you have to offer. Just like me, you do not shine for those who do not believe in you. With dignity you choose to meet people where they are at. The more one believes in you the more you reach out. Those that think you are too disabled are ignored, but accepted, no matter how frustrating it gets. I know this because I see that although most have not recognized who you are—and only your mom has recognized your potential—you still see life as a thing worth celebrating.

I am honored to be a part of your celebration.

Love Always, *Aunt Chris*

Finding Cory's Voice

by Aunt Chris

It would be some ten years later that I would be inspired to try to capture Cory's "celebration of life" in short stories to share with others. I had wanted to write a book about the contribution people with disabilities make to our world but I struggled with how to capture the real contribution that they make. Yes, there is the touchy-feely stuff like teaching us compassion and tolerance for difference, but it is so much more than that. It is more down to earth than that. It is more concrete. It is more complex—and has more to do with their abilities than their disabilities.

One problem is that to learn the deeper lessons that people with disabilities have to offer you need to connect with them. And the greater their level of disability the closer you need to get to make that connection. My nephew, Cory, is profoundly affected by multiple disabilities: mental retardation, cerebral palsy, blindness, and autism. What I have learned from Cory has come from my seeking to discover his take on the world around him as I assist him on a day-in-day-out basis with his personal care. As Cory's aunt I am not his primary caregiver; his mother, Nancy, is. The degree to which I learn the lessons Cory has to offer—the contribution Cory has to make to my life and the world—is the degree to which I am responsible for assisting him in interacting in that world.

Not everyone can provide for the day-to-day care of someone with a disability so the question became: How do I capture what I have gained from my work with Cory for those who don't have someone like Cory in their lives so that they can share the lessons I am learning?

The answer came from an unexpected place. The television was on one day as I was preparing something for Cory to eat. The show, *Crossing Over with John Edward*, was on in the next room and he was talking about people with disabilities. I heard him saying that when people with disabilities "cross over to the other side" they will no longer be disabled. Nancy, Cory's mom, and I agreed: wouldn't it be great to hear what Cory really thinks about things? How would he think we were doing in supporting him? (Yes, there was a little concern that we may not like everything he would have to say.)

Several months later, and in the middle of the night (when all good brainstorms happen!) it occurred to me: Let Cory tell his own story. When I got up that morning I wrote the first piece "A Quality Life by Cory Seiler as told by his Aunt Chris".

No matter what your spiritual beliefs I ask that when you read this collection of stories you open your mind to "Cory's perspective". In these pages I have tried to honor Cory as the unique individual that he is. As I write I ask myself to imagine Cory's spirit—without disability—a life chosen so that we could learn from him. I try to capture, not just his perspective as he deals with day-to-day life, but also the perspective of his higher self, his philosophies, the lessons he has learned, and the things he hopes others will learn from him.

I believe there is much to be gained by your imagining what a person like Cory thinks not just about getting through the day but about the greater things in life. Whatever your beliefs, I believe that entering into "Cory's world" as you read these pages will be a journey worth taking.

A Quality Life

by Cory Seiler as told by his Aunt Chris

I am profoundly affected by multiple disabilities including: mental retardation, cerebral palsy, and autism. I am also legally blind (totally blind in my right eye). This is not how I see myself but I begin in this way because most people see me as profoundly disabled and many people see my life as one not worth living.

Although I would not wish a disability on anyone, I want to share with you some stuff about my life hoping that you can expand your understanding of quality of life and perhaps enhance your own life through this understanding as those closest to me have.

I wake up each morning happy (usually) to see the day. I wake up with the sun. (My Mom sometimes wishes I would sleep-in a little.) I love the sun—and light. I can see differences in light and although my speech is very limited I often try to pull those closest to me into conversation about lights. I ask them "whaz zat?" and they look to see what I am pointing toward and when they say "light" I laugh.

That reinforces them for getting it right. I have taught those closest to me to label a number of things in my environment in this way—and usually they get things right—and I laugh.

Because of my limited speech I have had to teach my supports how I like things done by doing a lot of pointing and making sounds—and sometimes by getting mad. They now know that I have a rule about doors: they need to be closed all the way or open all the way—and what is open always needs to be open and what is always closed needs to be closed. Now if I see a cupboard door open and can't get to it myself I can point to it and grunt and they will close it for me. I thank them by saying, "Wuuunderrr"—another reinforcer I learned to use to teach them. I learned this from my mom. She would always say, "Wonderful" when I was learning things from her. It made me feel good so I now use it with my supports to make them feel good when they do something I like. It is important to make people feel good.

I was talking about how important light is to me. I like to sit by windows, I like to point to my shadow—and make people talk about it: "Whaz zat?" And, weather permitting, I like to sit out on my patio in my rocker. There again I can point to things and see if my family can label them.

I love it outside. I love the feel of the sun, and, when it happens, the breeze—although if it's too breezy I ask for a sweater: "coze on". Sometimes I don't really want a sweater, I am just engaging in conversation. Because of my limited speech my supports need to pay close attention to me to try to figure out what I really want. If they pay close attention they usually do pretty well.

Probably my most favorite thing is going for long rides in the car—preferably with the windows down! My mom's new car has automatic windows so she has taught me to open my own window. Sometimes she regrets this because I open the window even when she has air conditioning on. Although, all she has to do is tell me that it's too hot and close it herself and I'm okay with that. I probably could learn to close the window myself, although it is more difficult to do that—and frankly I'm not really very motivated to do so. From my perspective the window is better down; hot or cold, I love it.

Cory on the go

Back to my love of long rides—I find long rides relaxing. They are like therapy for me. As I begin them I still may be a little anxious because I am wondering (and worrying) how far we'll be going—I'm hoping we'll be going for a long ride. Eventually I just settle in and relax. When the car stops as we are riding along I always check to see if my window is still down because I do not feel the wind anymore. Then my Aunt Chris will remind me that we are stopped at a traffic light. (My Aunt Chris tolerates heat better than my Mom so I am more likely to get to have the windows down when Aunt Chris is driving. Aunt Chris loves to have the windows down too.)

Another thing I love to do is go exerwheeling at the malls. When I was in school the teachers thought I would not be able to learn to run a manual wheelchair that wasn't adapted to be operated by my left side only because I couldn't use my right side very well. But my mom wanted me to get a manual chair for that very reason.

She believed it would be good for me to learn to work my two sides together. I have memorized my way around our malls. At two-story malls I'm sure to hit all the elevators. I love going up and down. Anyway, it has been years now that I have been exerwheeling at the malls. People at the malls have come to expect me.

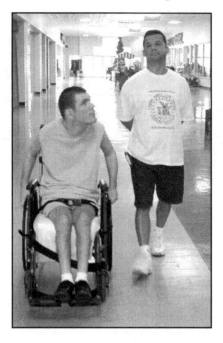

Cory exerwheeling at a mall with Uncle German.

Sometimes mall employees or other exercisers say hi as I wheel by. One mall employee even took the time to learn how to get me to say hi back. (If someone puts their hand on my shoulder and sticks around long enough I will say hi back.) Saying "hi" has been something my mom and supports have been working on with me. It is really hard for me to say hi in response to someone saying hi to me. First I have to notice they're talking to me because I can't see them (that's why the hand on my shoulder helps). Then I have to search for the right word. (Sometimes I say "Co-y" instead of "hi" because that is another word I have learned.) Then I have to say it loud enough for people to hear. Usually by the time I get it out people have pulled away because they don't want me to feel pressured. Or they may be saying a kind word just as I say "hi" but I haven't spoken loud enough for them to hear me through their words. Fellow exercisers at the mall will probably never hear me say hi back because they say hi and wiz on by. I don't mind. I am glad they say hi and pleased to just keep wheeling myself. I do sometimes say "hello." Saying "hello" is another word that I just came up with on my own (that bewilders my mom) and my supports picked up on this and have been working on this with me.

I have what some call echolalic speech. That is: I repeat the words I hear. You will often hear me say, "Are you done?" I am repeating a phrase I have heard a million times. (It originated in my early days of toilet training. You fill in the blanks.) Sometimes when I say this it seems to fit the context of the situation—like waiting in a check-out lane. I don't really mean to be rude. I have found too that this phrase works well to communicate that I need help with something or that I want something to be different—or to end or go away. Sometimes my family and supports work really hard to figure out what I mean. Sometimes people think I just said it because I can.

Probably one of the most embarrassing times to my mom is when she has to take me into the ladies room to go to the bathroom and I say loudly in my deep male voice, "Are you done?" Sometimes ladies reply from stalls, "Not yet!" probably thinking I am a maintenance man. This is the phrase I say most clearly. My female caregivers would probably prefer I say "hello" more clearly!

Again saying "hello" is something I have been working on. In the beginning my Aunt Chris decided that perhaps I would increase my use of the word "hello" if I heard it more often. This is sort of complicated to explain, but stay with me. First my Aunt Chris noticed how she and other supports pick up on what I say and copy me—they repeat my words and even my intonations. It is similar to what happens when adults interact with babies who are learning to talk—it just happens—no one intends to do it. For example, my Aunt Chris would find that when she was showering me she would respond to my repeatedly saying, "Are you done?" by singing, "Are you done? Are you done? Are you done?" to a familiar tune. Aunt Chris doesn't usually sing when she is showering herself so she cannot be expected to be too creative! She doesn't know why she sings when she is showering me. Anyway, first it occurred to her that she was probably reinforcing my "all-doning" (That is what we have come to call my frequent use of the phrase.) when she made a song of it. Then it occurred to her that perhaps it would be better to reinforce my use of the word "hello." I had said "hello" on occasion but wasn't using it regularly and she thought people may prefer hearing a "hello" rather than a "Are you done?" (Once I may have intimidated a government official at a public forum by clearly and loudly saying, "Are you done?" He may have preferred a "hello.") Anyway, now if Aunt Chris finds herself singing she will quit singing the "all-done song" and start singing her "hello, Cory song". That's as creative as she is going to get!

Anyway, I've been doing pretty well learning to say "hello." I will say it when I am leaving the house to go exerwheeling. Am I warming up in anticipation of seeing people in the community? I haven't really gotten to the point where I will say hello as other people do. I more or less throw my "hello" out there and sometimes a passerby will respond. Being legally blind and autistic I'm poor at eye contact so how much people respond to me has more to do with their familiarity with people with disabilities. Those who have been around people with disabilities are more likely to come up and talk to me. Some others may smile and move on, and others just look and turn away.

This is why my mom has made it her mission in life to get me out into the community. By getting me out in the community and allowing people to experience people with disabilities we both contribute to making this world a better place. Individuals without disabilities have reported that knowing someone with a disability changes their life perspective.

I guess one thing I do that I understand most people don't do is live life in the present moment. I don't spend time worrying about what I did yesterday. (Although I do freak out sometimes with doctors because doctors can do a lot of touching and moving you and I have no way of anticipating or understanding what is going to happen. To be honest, even if I understood, I do not like being touched.) I don't react to pain or smells or other things the way others do so people think I don't experience things at all. Well I do. People don't think I am capable of having a perspective so they don't try to imagine what my perspective might be. For example, when I need to get my blood drawn, people have a tendency to restrain me for 30 minutes while they prepare things—well maybe not 30 minutes but it feels like it from my perspective! Fortunately, some folks have listened to my mother and learned that it is not the needle that I mind so much; it is the restraint. So, if they get everything ready and only restrain at the necessary moment I may even get through it without a complaint.

Anyway, okay, I guess trauma I hold on to. But, for the most part I live in the present moment. I don't worry about the mistakes I made yesterday and I don't fear what is going to happen tomorrow.

I remember when I totally lost sight in my right eye. I noticed that it seemed like I wasn't seeing out of that eye so I decided to check this out with my mom. I covered my left eye and asked my mom

"Whaz at?" and pointed toward the light. My mom said, "That's the light." But, I couldn't see the light. I didn't think, "Oh, my God, what's going to happen to me now?" Instead I took in the new information and adapted. From then on when playing peek-a-boo I only needed to cover my left eye. It's all a matter of perspective.

I don't need to spend time imagining how horrible it would be to become disabled or to grow old and have to live in a nursing home and depend 100% on others to care for me. I am already dependent on others for my care. And my quality of life is in direct relation to the quality of my supports—both family and paid supports. I am fortunate; those closest to me have a value for assisting me in having the fullest life possible with the activities and things I love.

Those closest to me recognize how much I get out of participating in everyday activities as much as I can—like opening and closing the microwave door and pushing the on button with assistance. I may need help doing a lot of things but it makes me feel good to do whatever I can. As we all do—I love to make things happen. Things may take longer when I take part in them but I appreciate being able to contribute. It makes me feel good about myself.

My mom is often looking at the world through my eyes. For example when she goes shopping she is automatically looking out for anything that may be useful to me. A few months ago she spotted a CD player that was set up in such a way that I could possibly learn how to work it myself. (You know how complicated some of those things can get!) She told my Aunt Chris who told my grandma and grandpa and they all pitched in and bought me an early Christmas present. Well, just last week I turned on a CD all by myself. It made me feel so good I couldn't stop smiling. My Aunt Chris ran to get a camera and I was still smiling. Just yesterday I turned it on when no one was in the room. My mom had suggested, on a lark, that I go turn it on. I figure soon I will be turning it on myself whenever

I decide I want to—like I do when I want to play my keyboards. So far I like being able to share the experience with the people I love and who love me.

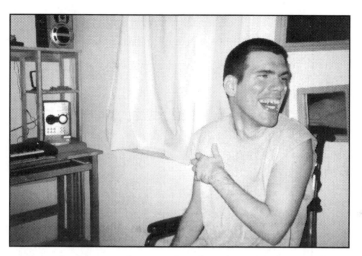

Cory the first time he turned on his CD player by himself.

I have not mentioned that I can be self-abusive and my pounding and some other behaviors can be destructive. Usually this happens when I do not understand what is happening to me. Routine helps me deal with that by helping me predict what will be happening to me. And when there is a break from routine (from what I expect to happen next) I get upset. I also can get upset when people seem upset around me; I think they are upset with me. If my mom gets upset with herself because she dropped something, I will get self-abusive. Then she will tell me that it's okay and I will calm down.

People close to me have learned that I hate going backwards. I am not sure why this is but my mom says it's vestibular. My Aunt Chris explains it this way: Because I have this uncanny ability to know where I am going when we go for rides even though I am legally blind, she figures that somehow my brain is able to keep track of where I am going—that is as long as I am going forward.

She describes my going backwards as a tape rewinding in my head; it screws up my unique locating ability. I can sometimes tolerate going backwards—in routine situations like pulling out of a parking stall and sometimes for a very short distance when I have been warned. This gives me time to get my head ready. It's a theory; I don't know.

My life is really pretty great. I am surrounded by people who love me, who laugh with me, who assist me in experiencing the sights, sounds, smells, flavors, and textures of this world as much as my senses allow.

Experiencing texture can be tough for me. They call this tactile defensiveness. I don't like to touch a lot of things and, as mentioned above, I am not always thrilled with people touching me. Still, through pottery class at a community art center I have learned to be comfortable touching clay and feeling the different textures I make — and, I'm making some new friends. And, I have a massage pad at home that I love. Also, my physical therapist has started massaging my hands and feet and I am beginning to enjoy that—plus it decreases my pounding.

I may not see like others but I love lights, shadows, and my reflection. I have great hearing and love music—as well as the sounds of motorcycles (now that's funny!) and airplanes. I don't like thunder much. I don't react to smells like others if you stick something by my nose. Only I know if I smell the popcorn that I hear popping. I love popcorn. That gets us into flavor. For a while I had to get fed through a tube in my stomach. I like it better now that I can eat again. Although I like to eat pretty much everything, I do appreciate that my mom will allow me to experience new and exotic foods just like someone without a disability even though I would never know what I was missing.

My experience of life is very full; it just isn't the same as yours. I appreciate and enjoy things you don't notice—and things you take for granted. People who don't get to experience life along with a person with disabilities can often find themselves spending their lives focused on unimportant things—things that don't contribute much to a quality life. Quality of life is about perspective. If you ask me, I'm living the good life.

Inclusion/Exclusion: Special Programs and Places for Grandma, Grandpa, and Me

By Cory Seiler as told by Aunt Chris

My mom is a big proponent of something called inclusion for people with developmental disabilities like I have. She has said, "I'll put Cory into a day program the day I go into one!" My Aunt Chris laughed, saying, "That could be sooner than you think!" implying that both my mom and my Aunt Chris are getting old.

They have been focusing a lot lately on getting old because they have been struggling to support my grandma and grandpa who are 82 years old; this has them doing a lot of thinking about what it will mean for them to get old—especially with me. My Aunt Chris had a dream once that our whole family moved into a very fancy assisted living facility. It was very spa like. We were given very plush white robes and towels for entering the pool area. Aunt Chris welcomed the idea of someone taking care of all of us.

People who don't have disabilities hate the thought of becoming so old that they are dependent on other people for support—in even the most personal of tasks. A lot of people avoid thinking about that reality even though my grandma's insurance agent says that 50% of people will end up in a nursing home. My grandpa always said, "When I get to that point take me to the bridge so I can jump." My grandpa has been in rehab several times. It was located in one wing of a nursing home. He hated being there (although he was glad to get the services he needed). He wanted to be out were people were living life.

I think that is what my mom wants for me—to be out living life—to the fullest. That is why she is so adamant that I participate in my community in the same ways that people without disabilities participate. No "special" programs for me—although I do need someone to assist me in my activities in the community 100% of the time.

I don't know if people fear having to go into a nursing home because they will be dependent on others for their care or because they will be "put away"—away from their homes, friends, family members, and community. Again, I can see why my mom believes so strongly in inclusion. If people without disabilities don't want to be put into nursing homes and day programs why would people with disabilities?

Now I know that there are a lot of activities that are targeted to seniors. I went to a big senior fair once with my grandma and Aunt Chris. Although a lot of stuff was about medical information for seniors, I enjoyed the music and seeing all the stuff and people. (I do like to go to new places.) Anyway, having activities that target certain age groups for people to choose from is not a problem.

My mom had me try going to country line dancing at a local bar because she figured that is what someone my age would be doing if they weren't disabled—and I like country music. As it turned out I loved going to the club. Although I couldn't get into the dancing because of the level of my disability, I love listening to the music (I do have some favorites now) and I just really get into the whole atmosphere. The lights are great and the music is loud. It is not the same as listening to my CD player at home. And people have come to expect me there. Folks that know me say hi and often new people come up and talk to me and my supports. (I wonder if they are just extra friendly or if they know someone with a disability so they are more comfortable talking to someone with a disability.)

Anyway, targeting activities toward seniors is not a problem. But, you can't do the same for people with disabilities. We are a very diverse group with varying interests, concerns, and ages! The trick is to try to find out what a person with a disability would like to do given all the possibilities in the world—not just the ones you have seen other people with disabilities do.

What has been the struggle for my mom has been to try to figure out what I really would like to do. First of all I can't talk, so we cannot talk about things I may want to try so my mom has to get me out just to try stuff to see if I like it. My mom tries real hard to see all the possibilities in this world. So often people are limited by the experiences they and those close to them have had. (For example, downhill skiers are more likely to come from families who went downhill skiing.)

Once my mom thinks of something I could try she needs to figure out how I am going to try it. Traveling to see new sights is not a problem for me (although my supports need to always be concerned about accessibility). However, trying to participate in new things is a problem for me. It's not that I don't want to try new things; I love expanding my world. However, when I try something new I am not exactly sure what I am supposed to do, and that freaks me out and I get self-abusive. My supports have figured out that they need to break tasks down to something I can do almost independently (that is without their needing to keep their hands on me [I hate people touching me] for more than a few seconds to show me what to do). If not, I may yell which seems like I am complaining about the activity. But, then I will reach out to do it again. My mom wonders if I am concerned that other people's expectations will be too high, or whether I am just too much of a perfectionist or both. I sure am glad my mom and my Aunt Chris never give up on me.

I can make teachers and therapists and new supports pretty uncomfortable with my yelling and self-abuse. Unfortunately, my getting upset usually gets them to increase the amount of time they keep their hands on me to guide me through something or they will try to rush through something to get it over with—with their hands on me which doesn't work and they lose hope. But my regular supports get excited at each little step I take toward participating in my environment. They have been with me for a long time and are in this for the long hall so the many little steps they have seen me master create a picture for them that is about me becoming me. Supports that come and go don't get to see the big picture so it is not so rewarding for them. Anyway, trying new things can be scary for me and my supports, but can also be very rewarding. It is all worth it. It's all good.

The Pottery Gang

by Cory Seiler as told by his Aunt Chris

My experience with clay began in my high school years. My mom had worked long and hard to get me into my regular neighborhood school and one of the results of that was that I was able to take art classes with "regular" high school students—kids without disabilities. (You see in reality we are all pretty "regular" whether or not we are disabled; and we are all pretty "special" whether or not we are disabled—but that's another story.) One of the things I worked with in art class was pottery. I even got to be a part of the school's art exhibit at the local mall. We had some very good artists in my school.

We moved to another state after I graduated (another story) and my Mom needed to find ways for me to continue what I had begun in high school. First we tried an art program for people with disabilities in a neighboring community. They did different types of art and had a small shop at the front of the building that displayed some of the art that was for sale. My mom would take me there and pick me up. I wasn't ever able to make something there to show my mom. Maybe they didn't know how to get me involved because of my level of disability; I don't know. I do remember that I couldn't wheel around because another guy, less disabled than I, would push me aside and put my brakes on. When my mom heard about this she decided it was time for me to learn how to take my brakes off! (That is now my responsibility; when I am done being transferred I am the one that releases my brakes.)

My mom used to come in to visit sometimes when she dropped me off or picked me up. Then, more and more, staff would be there to greet us outside when we arrived, and at the end of the day staff would have brought me outside to meet my mom before she arrived to pick me up. My mom pulled me out of that program because she couldn't tell what I was doing with my day.

Some time later my mom tried another program. She was very hopeful because this one talked about being an inclusive program. My mom and I would take the bus (1 ½ hours each way) to be a part of this program. (For some reason they were not able to provide the transportation they had promised in the beginning.) This program did not provide personal care for me so my mom found she had to be there to do that. They had artists do a project with everybody. Everyone worked on the same project. My mom most recalls the seascape painting project where we were being told how to paint sea oats. Right away my mom thought about how I am legally blind and I probably haven't seen sea oats—at least not as others do. This project would have little meaning to me even if I did have the fine motor skill to paint what they were instructing—and I don't. The few activities they did do that allowed their participants with disabilities to be a part of the community did not include me. My mom pulled me out of this program too.

Finally, my mom was able to find something that worked! We went to visit an art center—a regular old art center where regular old artists display their art and teach and take art classes. My mom talked to the education director who was very receptive and recommended a pottery class taught by Don. Don is an artist who makes these "guy sculptures" and does Raku. Don is now one of what we call the "pottery gang". Don was really great right from the beginning. I could tell he felt comfortable about my being a part of his class. At the beginning of each session when he would ask the class participants to introduce themselves; he would always have something additional to say about me that underscored how much I was a part of the class—I was a "regular". (Funny, I never thought about this before—being a "regular" means being one they come to expect. So what does this say about being "special"?)

Another "regular" in the class was Connie. Her specialty as an artist is these clay creatures she creates. Each one is unique and somehow loveable. My mom says, "They always make me feel good when I look at them." Connie has a great sense of humor and she and Don make a great team to listen to. There is also Tom. He does Eastern inspired work. He adds even another dimension to the laughter in pottery class. These are the members of the core pottery gang but there were many other regulars that came to know me, talk to me, and be a part of my experience at the art center. I ran into one pottery class member when I was visiting my grandpa in the hospital—small world. (There is a tendency for people to remember me even though I don't usually do much interacting with them. My mom and Aunt Chris have noted that often people recognize them because they recognize me first.) All these people made my pottery experience something important to me.

In the beginning, as with all new things, I was nervous about what was expected of me. I watched and listened to all the people.

They seemed happy—although at their first class everyone was quiet at first. I thought, "This can't be too bad. No one is complaining; no one is upset." I cautiously watched and listened; people seemed to be enjoying themselves—enjoying working with clay.

That first class my mom had brought my pottery tools from my high school days. After Don did his intro Mom reintroduced me to the rolling pin. I remembered how to use it so I got started right away but I didn't go too long—I was still nervous about what was expected of me. My mom gave me breaks as I chose, and I would return to using the rolling pin as I chose. I really didn't like the rolling pin. Then Don came over and suggested using a slab roller. All I can say is "Wonder! What an invention." I could roll a slab in a matter of minutes by turning this wheel—something I love to do anyway! I haven't gone back to using the rolling pin since. This allowed me to spend more time exploring other things I can do with clay.

I should say that I can only partially participate when working with clay. For example, to roll a slab my supports need to first cut me a chunk of clay of the right size. Then they place the clay on newspaper on my lap setting it up so that it won't fall off. Then I can wheel the clay to the slab roller. Once I get to the slab roller my supports need to take the slab from my lap and place it appropriately on the slab roller (and place the canvas as it needs to be). Finally, I can spin the wheel! When it is done (and I usually can feel that it is) I wait until my supports prepare the slab to be run through again sideways.

There are other things I learned to do over the course of several months. I could create different textures in the clay by rolling it between different kinds of fabric, (or rolling in a doily or something interesting), or hammering the slab with a meat mallet, or pressing stamps my mom and Aunt Chris made especially for my hands. I could cut shapes with cookie cutters my mom would find that my hand could manage—or use a pizza cutter. Sometimes I would just lay my slab on a drape mold and after it was dried and fired I could do neat things with glazes. (I did some draping in high school.)

One of Cory's spaghetti bowls with spaghetti pen holder.

My specialty at this point is the "spaghetti bowl". No, it is not a bowl for spaghetti. I make my spaghetti bowls from clay from a small extruder. My supports do the extruding for me because I do not have the fine motor skills to load or work the extruder myself. I hold my hand out waiting for the clay "spaghetti" to come out and then I place the spaghetti either in or over a mold depending on what I am making. I have made both bowls and pen/notepad holders using this method. For a different look I have done the same type of thing with clay balls. My Aunt Chris would make little balls for me and then I would place them in the molds.

I have done some work with glazing too. First I tried painting on low fire glazes. Yes, I could participate in doing some painting with the use of rollers and paintbrushes with special handles. But, it wasn't very easy for me. And, to top it off, I needed to put on many coats. I couldn't even see the difference as I added each new coat to experience that I was accomplishing anything. So, then I gave the high fire glazes a shot because you just dip pottery pieces in buckets of glaze. My supports would dip a piece to get a base color. Then I would paint on a second color. Or I could drizzle or pour on a second color. Or I could sponge on another color. This worked much better especially if there was high contrast between the base color and the color I added over it so I could see. I would have to get my face real close to see what I had done.

I really appreciate being able to do all this stuff even though I require so much help to get any one thing completed. It is hard to explain and hard to express my gratitude for being able to participate in these things as best I can. And, I hope that my family and supports recognize my appreciation by noting my interest when I bend down close to see how I've impacted my environment in every little way that I do. It would be very easy for me to sit back and rock my life away. Rocking is one of my "self-stims". (That's short for "self-stimulating behavior"—something common to people with autism but other people have them too. My grandpa used to wiggle his big toe.) I would be in my own little world and people could just ignore me. But, instead I get to make color appear on pottery. Even with my limited vision I want to see what I made happen! I really appreciate having that opportunity. I really appreciate how they are helping me.

Another thing that pottery class has given me is the opportunity to work through some of my defensiveness about touch. I used to hate touching things. Now you can catch me reaching out to touch the texture I have put on a slab of clay. You couldn't get me to even touch the clay in the beginning—ick!

Probably what I got the most out of in pottery class though was being a real part of a wonderful group of people now affectionately called the pottery gang.

Don, the teacher would share with me materials that he thought I'd be interested in checking out. He'd ask my mom or other supports about me since I cannot tell him things myself. He'd always get excited when he would hear me say a word or phrase he had not heard me say before. He would frequently touch base with me in small ways that made me feel I was a part of the class while not taking away from the class as a whole. On days when there were only a few people in class Don would sit next to me and talk to me about things. He would try to imagine my perspective on things. He thinks I have a pretty good perspective on things. I had been working on saying "hi" and Don would take the time to work with me on this. At one point I was even working on saying "Don" but that was hard. "Don" is a lot like "Done", a word I say a lot, ask any member of the pottery gang!

Connie also got excited when she would hear me say something she hadn't heard before. You should have seen these folks when I brought my communication device into pottery class. They began by listening to all that I could say when I pressed the buttons. Then one day after discussion about how the voice they had to hear me speak with was my mom's or my Aunt Chris', they did some recording of their own voices. First, Tom offered to be my voice on some of the buttons. Then we set up a page for fun and each pottery gang member recorded a funny thing on a button or two. Connie made the buttons say "Go Bucs!" and "I want to go to Grandpa's". (During one session we often went to my Grandpa's after class.) Don mad the buttons say "Hi, I am Cory and you are not!" and "I want to have some broccoli please". (One of the pictures he found on the device looked more like broccoli than whatever it was supposed to be.) When I am at home I often go to my pottery gang page and push their buttons just to hear their voices—they make me smile.

Don no longer teaches at the art center so the pottery gang decided to meet at a local health food store/restaurant to talk about what we could do next. We have met for lunch a couple times and talked about places to get together. We are still working on ways to stay connected and in the meantime I work on pottery at home and other members of the gang stay in touch by e-mail. I hope I am able to connect with the gang again and I hope that I am able to find places where I can connect to people in a similar way. It's good to feel a part of such a wonderful group of people.

★ *"Wonder" is a word I use often. I learned it when I was young when my mom would say I was wonderful as I was learning things. I now use it regularly to reinforce my supports when they do something I like. That way they know they got it right. I also use it to communicate that I am enjoying something and to compliment myself when I have done something I am proud of.*

The Line Dancing Gang

by Cory Seiler as told by his Aunt Chris

Yes, I know what you're thinking: How does a person who is profoundly affected by multiple disabilities (including cerebral palsy, autism, and legal blindness) get involved in line dancing?

Well, it's quite simple. I love listening to music—and although my taste in music is expanding (as new people introduce me to the joy they experience in listening to their kind of music)—country music is one of my favorites.

My love of country music goes back a long way. When I was three years old, my mom and my Aunt Chris were learning to play guitar and my mom would practice early every morning before she had to go to school. I would scoot underneath the guitar, lie there, and watch her strum the guitar—bouncing and kicking and enjoying myself. When I was able to do more sitting up my mom would set me up across from her and the guitar. She would fret the guitar and let me strum it while we played the songs that she was practicing.

The songs she played were country and folk music. My mom liked folk music, and folk and country songs were easier to play.

I would go with my mom and Aunt Chris to guitar lessons each week. The guitar instructor became our friend and one day he asked if we wanted to go with him to help set up for his band. The band played country music at clubs and jazz for fun. Anyway we went to help them. At that time I was scooting on my bottom to get around (when I wasn't in my chair) and that day while scooting around I began making this sound: "Chh-Chh-Chh, Chh-Chh-Chh, Chh-Chh-Chh". One of the guys in the band heard the rhythmic sound I was making, picked up on it, and began playing his instrument to go along with it. Then another member of the band heard what was happening and joined in. Pretty soon the whole band was playing music based on the little rhythmic noise I was making as I scooted along! As they got going I lost track of what I was doing and focused on the music they were creating. It was great!

I sort of became obsessed with the guitar. I hated it when my mom would quit playing. My mom says I have perfect rhythm. She is not sure if I always had it or if I picked it up with those early experiences with her guitar playing. My mom picked up pretty quickly that I loved music and she began right away looking for ways I could control music. She would look for radios I could turn on myself or that could be set up so that they could go on when I flipped the light switch. She worked with me on learning to say "on" so I could communicate that I wanted my radio on. She chose country radio stations because I liked rhythm and melody and because country music would be a safer bet (no offensive language) to have on all the time.

There was one rock song on the rock stations in those days that would make me cry—it wasn't so much music it was a lot of loud clapping sounds—very rhythmic but I didn't like it. My mom didn't want me to hear something that would make me cry. Also, I love it when people sing along to music. I have noticed that they seem to be happy when they sing along to songs. Country music was good for singing along.

There is one situation where (at least as a young boy) I did not like people singing along—that is singing happy birthday. For years I would cry when people would sing happy birthday. My mom and Aunt Chris thought maybe I associated the birthday song with some bad memories. Another theory was that people are likely to be off key and out of sync—you have to admit people really don't concern themselves with how they sound when they sing happy birthday!

There is one more type of music that makes me cry—Christmas carols. But, this is a good cry; I love Christmas carols. One of my favorite things to do during the Christmas season is to go for a long ride looking at Christmas lights and listening to Christmas music on the radio.

That reminds me—just this last year for Christmas my mom found me a CD player that was set up in such a way that I could work it myself. It took several months for me to learn but now I am able to turn it on and select from among 5 CD's totally by myself. But, that's only listening to music at home. There is more to music than that!

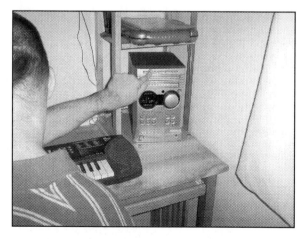

Cory turning on his CD player.

My mom thought that being a young man in my twenties (Now I am an old man of thirty—but that's another story.) I should be getting out and doing what other guys my age are doing. Well, one of those things is going out and enjoying "the night life". She found out about a group of folks who were doing country line dancing at a local club. They had line dancing lessons for a couple hours before traditional opening time. First my mom went to check out the situation. She thought she would enjoy learning to line dance herself. Once there she concluded that I might really enjoy the music and atmosphere so she told my Aunt Chris to bring me in to see if I would like it. That was two years ago. Now they have come to expect me there!

The line dancing gang consists of Anne, the instructor who is also president of the Country Line Dancing Association and a large group of up to 80 people who follow Anne around to various locations. (Because of clubs closing the group has had to move frequently throughout the last couple years). The group consists of young and old, beginners and more advance dancers. Often a group of dancers will join Anne in dance competitions across the country. We've had a number of winners from our very own group. I join the group for beginners' night and sometimes Saturday night for the mixed group where they have just a short lesson and then lots of dancing.

My participation in this group has evolved through the years. When I first started my supports would be greeted as we came through the door and paid the cover charge. Bouncers might help hold a door open so that we could get in. Anne always greeted everyone with a hug or a friendly hello and I was no exception. Over the course of time my mom introduced me to a number of dancers. What I enjoyed most about line dancing though was the music and the lights.

Cory watching dancers.

Due to my poor vision lights are important to me. I always try to get my supports to talk to me about lights. I point to them and say "loo" (look) or "whas a?" (What's that?) and they need to guess what I am pointing at and label it for me. It's something we do all the time. Anyway, there are a lot of different lights in nightclubs; it's great!

As time went on and I continued to go to line dancing each week, and as we changed locations, more and more people became familiar with me. More bouncers would help us get through doors and tell us to have fun. Other dancers would smile as we passed to go to our usual table. (Speaking of tables—now here was a table I could pound on and be "appropriate!" On occasion you could see others pounding away to the beat of the music!) People didn't seem fazed by my repeatedly saying, "Are you done?" throughout the dance lessons. Anne knew it was me and that "all done" is just one of the things I often say sometimes just because I can—or this time is it because I want them to quit the lesson and get going with the music? (Well, let me say this: I wouldn't mind if they got going on the music.) Anyway, everyone just keeps on dancing and I keep listening to the music. On occasion people have come up to talk to me personally. For short periods off and on we were at a location where the owner or manager greeted me personally at my first and later visits. At a different club another gentleman would come over to talk to me each time he came in. His name was Don (the same name as my pottery teacher). But, he and his wife were new to line dancing and with the change in locations I didn't see them again. Another lady who talked to me was also a new person and because of changing locations we may have lost her in the shuffle. Changing places can be troublesome to new people that don't feel they are a part of the group yet.

There was one club I especially liked. Our group was there for a long time and the lights were great and the people working there all knew everybody. People had parties there often. Often birthdays were celebrated there and people would bring cake to share with everyone. One dancer celebrated getting his doctorate with a big buffet! And, of course they celebrated the traditional holidays like New Year's Eve. What more can you ask for? Good food, good music, good people, and good lights!

Unfortunately, the owners of the club sold it and it was torn down. They had a big going away party and a newspaper reporter came to do a big story about it. Actually my picture got in the paper—but you can't really tell it's me. You can see my table and you can sort of see that there might be a person there—that's me! Anyway, one thing the newspaper did capture was the story of Debbie and Tom. They were a couple of line dancers that met at the club years ago and then married!

Debbie and Tom are great people and great dancers. They dance at the front of the group offering leadership on new dances or when a review is needed. They also have won a number of dance competitions. Most of all they are just great people.

One evening my Aunt Chris and I were heading back from a beach ride (another one of my favorite things) and cut through the apartment complex where my grandparents live. When we pulled into my grandma's parking spot Debbie and Tom pulled up right next to us on bikes all out of breath! Debbie explained while trying to catch her breath that she and Tom had thought they recognized me (my hand and probably head were hanging out the window) as we pulled onto the road that goes through the apartment complex. They raced their bikes through the entire complex praying that my Aunt Chris would stop so they could say hi. It's a good thing we did stop. They were really out of breath! We had not been able to have line dancing for a few weeks because of location problems, so it was great to see Debbie and Tom. My Aunt Chris talked to them for a few minutes about looking forward to the group getting set up in a new location.

People are really pretty great if we give them an opportunity to be that way. My Aunt Chris heard a story about a dad with a son who was disabled and it was this father's belief that everything that God creates is perfect and that people with disabilities are God's creation designed to bring out the perfection in others—like this experience with Debbie and Tom.

In the last few weeks I have returned to line dancing. (There had been some accessibility issues that needed to be worked out at our new location which is a dance studio.) First, let me say the lights are great! There are icicle lights all the way around the room and these grape lights that hang over a little bar/kitchen area. Anne runs the music from in there. There are also two full walls of mirrors (another favorite thing of mine). They have the effect of multiplying the lights! And, there is a disco ball in the center of the ceiling. (Yes, I have repeatedly pointed these things out to my supports and required that they label them.)

Anyway, Anne had called my mom to encourage me to come. (Everyone has given Anne their phone number so she can keep them informed of any changes in location.) Anne was working on possible ways to fit me in the very limited space of the studio. As it worked out I get a great seat right in front of the dance floor! Although my vision is extremely limited I was able to see Debbie and Tom just last week when they were wearing their black shirts. They were dancing their hearts away. Tom is very tall so he is easier to see anyway. They also lead in the hootin' and hollerin' so if I can't see them I can hear them. I can also learn when in the song I can expect to hear them. That makes it more fun! Anyway, I was really enjoying myself last week. Even on the way to line dancing I was bopping to the music on the radio in the car.

My Uncle German has been dancing with me to the music on my keyboard and since he is a really enthusiastic, fun guy, we really get into it and I can get my whole body bopping to the music. Although, usually I just bounce my left hand up and down and sometimes get my shoulders into it and/or I rock my head and arm back.

Cory Dancing

Anyway, I was really in the dancing mood last week. I was smiling while watching Debbie and Tom and the other dancers and on occasion I would be bopping my hand up and down to the music. At one point one lady came up and grabbed my hand lightly and started to dance with me. And, I smiled through the whole thing. There would have been a time that I would have pulled away and stopped listening to the music—not so much because I don't want people to touch me, but more because I am not sure what is expected of me. But, I just danced with this lady. Anne had announced earlier in the evening that that lady was one of the snowbirds who would be heading north. So, I won't be seeing this dance partner again for several months. I hope she comes back. I didn't even catch her name.

Another lady has made a point these last couple weeks of encouraging me to keep coming back. I don't know her name either. But, it seems that I was missed those weeks I wasn't able to go. And I know I missed being there.

I guess those positive interactions from others that come unpredictably, cannot be planned, and can only be given opportunity to happen are those things the father of the boy with the disability was referring to when he spoke of God's perfection.

Not Always Easy, But Always Worth It

by Cory Seiler as told by his Aunt Chris

I take the ups and downs of trying to connect with people in my community with stride. If people do not want to connect with me or if they feel uncomfortable when I am around it doesn't bother me in the least. Some people who reach out to me may be disappointed in my response. It takes some time for me to recognize that someone is talking to me. Then I have to recognize that they are looking for a response. Then I need to decide which response is appropriate. I have a small number of words that I have learned and sometimes I say the wrong one. Probably most often I don't even recognize that someone is talking to me. My caregivers know I value being around people so they are always thinking about how others see me.

My mom has a strong commitment to my being a part of my community. One thing she does is pay attention to clothing styles. When I was younger she would get me clothes like the other kids

were wearing. Now that I am older nice clothes do the job. (I do have a T-shirt from one of the line dancing conferences I attended. And I used to have one with a hurricane on it from when our area almost got hit by a huge hurricane.) She also works hard at setting me up for success in the community. She knows how nervous I can be when I am not sure what is expected of me so she introduces me to new situations gradually. She wants me to experience success and she wants people in the community to have a positive experience too.

My Uncle German will worry about my being rejected by people in the community, but he has learned to tell himself to let it go. He used to worry most about it at restaurants because I pound on tables. (No one is fond of my pounding but for me it is a way of checking out my environment—Do you know how many restaurant tables are unstable in this world?—Nearly all of them!) My supports worry that some people will judge them for not punishing the pounding out of me. But, it can be disastrous to try to punish away a behavior that is used to serve a function without finding a better way to serve the same function. My fine motor skills, sight, and touch are not good at all, but I can get a lot of information from pounding.

All my supports know that the best way to handle my pounding is to address problems if there are any and then get on with assisting me in eating. With a little responding to my attempts to engage them in conversation about lights and my reflection in the table things soon work themselves out. Then, I like to relax quietly after I have eaten.

My Aunt Chris wrote about supporting me in line dancing and shared her story with other families. She believes that letting people know that they are not alone in being nervous about how others will accept their loved one with a disability will give them strength. And, the stories of successes will give them hope. There are usually

many more pleasant surprises than there are disappointments when connecting with others in the community.

The next story is what she wrote about supporting me at my first line dance conference.

Inclusion:
Feeling the Fear and Doing it Anyway

by Aunt Chris

This is the true confession of a person given the responsibility of facilitating inclusion at a national line dance conference for a person who is profoundly affected by multiple disabilities (a first for each of them).

Cory's mom, Nancy, described her anticipation of our attendance at the Line Dance Classic as "a good opportunity to get away from it all!" As I anticipated attending the conference my feelings were quite different. I was afraid.

Let me go back to the beginning—when Nancy talked to me about her vision, Cory having a night life like most men his age, I supported her value. When she told me she found a line dancing club where this could happen I was thrilled for Cory—though not enthused for myself having no real interest in country music or line dancing. And, it's always sort of scary to take Cory to a new place because people can react negatively to some of his behaviors, and sometimes they react negatively to his mere presence. But, as Cory's support person it wasn't about me—my fun or my fears—this was about Cory. It was about giving Cory an opportunity to experience some of the same things that a person without a disability would experience; it was about giving people in Cory's community an opportunity to experience life with Cory.

For a good year I dragged myself out to the club with Cory—I am no longer the night person I was in my younger days! People were friendly. Anne, the dance instructor, would greet everyone with a big hug. Bouncers would hold doors for us. People would stop and say hi. As time passed more people became familiar with Cory. Cory of course immediately loved the music and the lights. I think he got into the whole atmosphere—he knew this was special. (He knew this was "special" in a way "special" education never was.) Anyway, what I am trying to convey is that "including" Cory was a slow and not necessarily fun-for-me activity but it was important for Cory—really important for Cory—and that was my reward—at least in the beginning.

Then something wonderful happened. Cory wasn't able to attend line dancing anymore because the group had changed locations and there was limited space. As it turned out over the course of time people had come to accept Cory as part of the group and they didn't want him left out. Anne called to invite Cory to the new location. She had worked out an accessible spot for him right in front! Being in the front facilitated people connecting with Cory even more.

Several months later, Nancy would give me my next challenge. She wanted Cory to try dancing on the dance floor. (Cory had been dancing—bopping his hand and head to the music—on the side lines more and more. But he never danced out on the floor.) There is a rule in line dancing—line dancers stay to the center so couples can dance around the perimeter. My fears surfaced: "Where would Cory fit in? We already were doing a different dance to the song than most of the group. There is such limited space. What if people get annoyed at having to make room for Cory on the dance floor? What if Cory becomes self-abusive; what will people think?"

I didn't share my fears with Cory's mom. I figured it was just negative thinking that may discourage her and, anyway, it wouldn't be fair to Cory for me to not give him an opportunity to experience something because I am afraid people won't be nice about it. I followed Nancy's lead, so when she said, "Let's try it," we got out on the dance floor and danced. (Of course first we figured out how Cory could do the dance in his home in a wheelchair and practiced with him.) And Cory did it! Cory reacted positively to the new experience and so did the group.

Before we knew it we were participating in the dance competition at the Line Dance Classic. Again my fears were surfacing, but at the same time everyone was being so supportive, and people were connecting more and more with Cory. Again I did not share my fears with Cory's mom. I just kept adjusting my attitude—telling myself to quit worrying about things that haven't happened.

I had the additional issue of performance anxiety but was inspired by what Jennifer Lopez said to Richard Gere in the movie *Shall We Dance*. She explained that in dancing the man is the frame for the woman; it is his job to make her look good [she said it much more eloquently] and I thought, "This is true for Cory and me too. When I dance with Cory (I am pushing his wheelchair) I am his frame—it is about him; it is my job to make him look good". So I told myself to get over my fears and do the best that I could to make him look good. It occurred to me that this is always the case when you are supporting someone with a disability—whether you are a natural support or a paid support; it is your job to make the person with the disability look good—look "includable"—you are his or her frame.

My fears returned again once at the hotel. The hustle and bustle of preparing for the event as well as meeting Cory's needs helped me maintain my focus and distracted me from my fears until, without Cory, I found myself riding down in the elevator. I was listening to the folks going down with me greeting each other. It was clear that they were line dancers who knew each other from previous events. I felt like such an outsider. Again the negative thinking: "What if they have a problem with Cory being here? He's isn't really line dancing; I have to push him. I can't really line dance myself—not well enough to be attending a line dance conference. What if they don't like us intruding in their world? What if Cory gets self-abusive?" As we reached the ground floor I heard myself say, "Feel the fear and do it anyway." (This was the title of a book written by a woman I heard speak probably ten years ago—Susan Jeffers, Ph.D.) And I did just that, I felt the fear and did it anyway.

Friday night, all dressed up, we waited with the other competitors in the hall. It was quite a mix of people. Cory was the only one in a wheelchair. People treated us like we were just another competitor—although people were kind to ensure we could get into the room through the crowd. People were mostly focused on their own performance anxiety. Then it was our turn.

Our performance was great! Well I don't really know what our performance was like but people's reception of Cory was great. As a matter of fact, because Cory "dared" to be a participant in the competition, people connected more with Cory over the next couple days. The night before people had accepted Cory's presence there and folks from our local line dance gang made a point to connect, but after the competition people were coming out of the woodwork to connect with Cory or share stories about how they have a family member with a disability. Some just wanted to say how pleased they were that Cory seemed to really enjoy dancing. Young men would make a point of holding doors open. Cory was no longer the person with the disability in the crowd; he was a fellow line dancer.

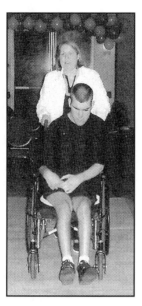

Cory and Mom dancing at his second line dance conference.

I can't express how good that made me feel about people—and how glad I was that I was willing to "feel the fear and do it anyway". If I hadn't, Cory would have lost out on a wonderful opportunity. But, worst of all I would have gone on feeling the fear of rejection when I had nothing to fear at all.

I am sure I will again feel the fear of rejection for Cory. Cory has been rejected by people repeatedly. It always hurts—deep in my heart. But, I will again "feel the fear and do it anyway" for Cory—for me—for all of us.

And, more often than not, I will be reminded that people are more likely to welcome Cory than to turn him away.

Christine T. Seiler, PhD

Supporting Cory forces me to question the voice in my head that keeps me worrying about what other people will think. I may well avoid facing my fears if it were only about me. But, when it is about Cory I can't let worries about things that haven't happened yet stop me from helping him try something new. Cory forces me to face my fears so that I can learn that they were not warranted. Experiencing the goodness in people decreases my fear and increases my trust in humankind. It puts me in touch with a reality that is out there—it is my fear that is unreal.

Feel the fear and do it anyway® is a registered trademark of Susan Jeffers, PhD and is used with her permission.

Going to School with Kids like Cory

by Aunt Chris

Very young children are often curious about Cory and his wheelchair. Cory's much younger cousin used to enjoy playing in his wheelchair all the time.

Once when Cory was exerwheeling at the mall a toddler who had been distracted by Cory's wheeling past was not responding to her mother's and then grandmother's calls. I commented with a chuckle that she found Cory too interesting to leave behind for the moment. Both the mother and grandmother just looked at Cory and me with troubled looks that I am now not finding the words to describe—although the experience is familiar. Neither said a word to us in response; neither smiled. And, I concluded that neither of them had had previous experience with someone like Cory before. I thought to myself, "If this mom and grandma had had the opportunity to go to school with someone like Cory this wouldn't have been such an uncomfortable situation for them."

This experience stood in sharp contrast to one that we had a few days previously, when Cory and I were going through a drive-through. The girl, after handing me our food, made a point of extending to Cory. As I stumbled around trying to get my change back in my purse she yelled a friendly hello over to Cory. Surprised, I stopped what I was doing and encouraged Cory to say hi back (with no luck). As I moved on, allowing the car behind us to get its order, I noted that Cory looked happy enough and I trusted the girl was okay with his lack of response.

As I drove off I wondered if she perhaps had gone to school with someone like Cory. I recalled Cory's middle and high school years when Cory was included in general education classes.

Because Cory is profoundly affected by multiple disabilities (including mental retardation, cerebral palsy, and autism), if it weren't for the significant effort of his mother for all of his school years he would have attended a separate school for kids with disabilities. During his elementary years he went to those schools. Then his mother began the fight to get him into his neighborhood school so that he could go to school with the same kids he was living around.

There are a lot of stories to share about those years when his mother fought for his right to attend his neighborhood school—and some wonderful stories of success.

The next story is about Cory's graduation. It is a story that still makes me cry.

A Graduation Story

by Aunt Chris

Cory, Mom, and Aunt Chris on graduation day.

I remember the first time I walked into Cory's middle school. It was in the evening, so the halls were dim and virtually empty and the lockers seemed to go on forever. I held back tears.

This was different. So different from the special programs I had become accustomed to as a special education aide and then teacher. Special education programs have a different feel to them. Yes, they are made up of lots of kids with disabilities and special equipment and puzzles and lots of primary colors and kid's stuff. But, there is also a lot of staff—and the staff, having worked together for years, get close and comfortable and in many ways it becomes their environment.

No way was Cory's middle school a "staff environment". I got the distinct impression when I walked in those door that this environment belongs to the hundreds of middle school kids that attend school here—no matter what the principal or teachers think! I was proud that Cory was one of the many kids that attended school there.

It was seven years later when Cory was graduating from his neighborhood high school. I remember walking from the parking ramp to the Civic Center with Cory, his mom, Nancy, and Cory's grandma and grandpa. We, along with hundreds of other families and students carrying gowns, walked quickly through the downtown streets. I had graduated from a Catholic school so we graduated in our school gym. This was a big deal. I thought, "So this is how it's done in regular school."

As usual, graduates had to gather in one area to prepare for the ceremony and guests needed to go find seating. We met up with Cory's Program Assistant (This was the person that assisted Cory through his school days in regular classes; she was Cory's "one-to-one".) She would stay with Cory and assist him through the ceremony. The rest of us had to go find seating, a struggle because Cory's grandpa was not able to handle the steps. We had to go find an elevator to get up to our section. It was a struggle but it all worked out and eventually we were seated—although it seemed like miles away.

We waited for the ceremony to begin. On one hand it was exciting as graduations are because they are a rite of passage and very important. On the other hand they aren't in and of themselves very entertaining—and this was a huge group of graduates. We waited.

Finally the ceremony began. There were all the speeches—and I must say that, after listening to all the speeches, I was left with the same sense of pride in America's education system and the kids that were coming out of it as I do at all graduation ceremonies.

Then, after the speeches and before handing out diplomas, they made the announcement. They asked that in the interest of time people not applaud after each person's name is called to come up and get the diploma. "No problem," I thought, "this is what drags these things out anyway". I listened as they called the first name thinking, "And, once again we have to wait for the S's."

The first name was called and family and friends applauded— breaking the rules. But there is one in every crowd right? Then another name was called. Applause again! And then the third, and then the forth. It seemed that everyone's family and friends were going to break the rules; everyone's family and friends were going to applaud and hoot and holler. My heart sank into the pit of my stomach. What about Cory?

There would be silence when Cory's name was called. We needed to break the rules; we had to applaud. But there were only the four of us and we were not the hooting and hollering kind. Would anyone hear our meager applause? I sat horrified at the thought that no one would be able to hear how proud we were of Cory and how important he was in our lives. I was afraid he would seem so alone—so without friends. I struggled with how I could get myself to make some noise. Maybe I could if I was part of a crowd, but no such luck. I would sound silly hooting and hollering by myself. I struggled with this silently as each name was called. Through the A's, through the B's, through the C's, through the D's, through the E's, through the F's, through the G's, through the H's, through the I's, through the J's, through the K's, through the L's, through the M's, through the N's, through the O's, through the P's, through the Q's, through the R's, and then came the S's.

I had decided that for Cory I needed to give it my best shot. I am a quiet person so I hoped I would be able to find it in me to make some serious noise. Then I heard his name, "Cory Seiler".

Before I could even get my hands together for that first clap I was drowned out by the Area High School class of '94. Cory got a standing ovation. Cory was wheeled up to the stage by his aide to get his diploma as the kids continued to applaud. I clapped and cried.

I was so proud not only of Cory but of those kids. What a world we are creating!

Cory's aside as told by Aunt Chris:

My Aunt Chris, after the ceremony, in the basement of the civic center where we students had gathered in preparation and were now doing things like taking photos, shared how afraid she was that there would be silence when my name was called. As it turned out my mom and grandma and grandpa had all felt the same way! They each struggled with how they would have to "break the rules". I don't worry about these things. I believe you need to give people the opportunity to come through and be glad when they do and figure they weren't ready when they don't. AND, be prepared to give them yet another opportunity.

Some people say life is a school and we are all here to learn. My attending my neighborhood school has not only increased my opportunities for learning, it has increased the opportunities for learning for all the other students and staff. I couldn't have made this contribution if my mom hadn't pushed so hard to have me "included". I appreciate her efforts more than she will ever know.

Being a Significant Other

by Aunt Chris

I am not Cory's primary caregiver. My sister Nancy is. At Cory's school meetings and doctor appointments Nancy would often describe me as Cory's significant other. I guess that means a really involved aunt.

Nancy has often expressed great appreciation for how I have been there for her and Cory through the years. It strikes me how appreciative she is of simply my presence by her side. Every time she mentions to someone how nice it is to have my support I am reminded how easy it is to be there for someone. It draws my attention to how much easier it is to be the significant other instead of the mom.

I find it a comfort to not be the primary decision maker. As mom, Nancy is responsible for all decisions. I can trust that Nancy has Cory's best interests at heart and this allows me to let go.

Everyone is looking to her for answers to their questions. I can go along for support. I can offer my opinion when asked but Nancy needs to decide what action to take. And, if I don't have a clue what action is best, I can say, "I don't know." She still needs to decide what to do.

And, sometimes we both understand that there are situations where one cannot know what the best course of action is. We have to trust that good intentions set a path that will somehow turn out to be as it should be. As Cory would say if he could, "It's all good."

Nancy tells a story of a time I heroically saved the day. When cutting Cory's hair once, she forgot to put a comb on the clippers. We both remember the occasion well. But, I in no way feel like anything heroic happened. She on the other hand was frantic. When she was telling me about her error she sounded as if she had maimed Cory for life. She explained, "After working so hard to help Cory fit in with his peers, look what I've done!" She had taken a big gouge out of his hair cut. She was beside herself. How does one put hair back on Cory's head? In heroic fashion (as she describes it) I came to her aide. The solution: I cut Cory's hair very short. A style he still wears today.

I was able to resolve the situation because I had no ownership in the mistake. Where a mom who makes a mistake may be screaming to herself, "What have I done to my child?" and immediately imagine horrible future scenarios her child is going to go through; a significant other such as myself enters the scene minus the feeling of horror (guilt?) and finds a solution.

How many kids—or adults for that matter—have had to endure a hair mistake or bad haircut? You can ask Cory's Uncle German. He will tell you of a day when I was cutting his hair. I took a gouge out of his cut and told him with complete confidence that it would grow back. My experience with Cory was a great lesson and Uncle German still lets me cut his hair. So, all is good!

I recall my being the primary caregiver on more than one occasion when Cory went into a rage. Cory's mom was gone and I couldn't figure out what was going on with Cory. One time Cory suddenly started throwing a tantrum while sitting on the commode. He kept banging his head on the ceramic tile wall so I put my hand between his head and the wall. He kept banging but I was alone with him, my cell phone was out of reach, and the wheelchair had rolled out of reach. I was afraid to remove my hand from his head because the sound of his head hitting the wall had me concerned he would do permanent damage. I knew he would be safer if I could get him to his bed. But as long as my hand was on his head I couldn't get the wheelchair back. My hand was getting banged up pretty bad as it remained the buffer between Cory's head and the ceramic tile wall. Not able to get to my phone I yelled as loud as I could for Cory's Uncle German. He has a way of making Cory smile even when he is not in the best of moods. Even if he can't pull Cory out of it, it is reassuring to have someone else there to take over for a few minutes so that I can regain my composure and remind myself that *everything will be okay*. Often we never figure out what happened to upset Cory. But Cory always works himself out of it. We just need to keep him safe. One can see why having a circle of supports—that is a few significant others—can be of great benefit.

Cory's mom has much more to say about Cory's bad haircut adventure because of the trauma it caused her. In the same way I have much more to say about Cory's rages than his Uncle German would. But, that is my point: As a significant other, contributions that you perceive as no big deal can be of tremendous value to the primary caregiver. And as we build a community expecting to have individuals like Cory as full participants we will also create more significant others who contribute in supporting moms, dads, and family members in ways in which they have yet to imagine.

Living the Life at 39

by Cory Seiler as told by his Aunt Chris

It has been eight years since I last wrote about my life and 18 years since I graduated from high school. A lot has happened since that time. I moved again to another state with my family.

My Grandpa had passed away just a little before we moved. But I know he is still with me. After Grandpa died I would sometimes point into the space in front of me and ask "What's that?" and laugh. My mom wondered if I could "see" Grandpa. Grandpa was the kind of guy that always made people laugh. He would make jokes all the time. He would take what was happening in the moment or who he was with and make up new words about it and find a song to sing that fit or a familiar tune to sing his own words. He was not always sure how to connect with me, but I knew he loved me. On our first Father's Day in our new home a flower popped up in the garden out of nowhere. My mom said it was Grandpa saying, "Hi!"

Was I seeing Grandpa when I pointed into the air in front of me? Was Grandpa making me laugh? Did Grandpa send us the flower? Sometimes questions are best left unanswered. If you think you need to always have the answers life can become pretty miserable. It is better to wonder about the possibilities. Possibilities are limitless.

Anyway, when we moved we combined three households (mine, my Aunt Chris', and my grandma's) so that everyone could work together to help support Grandma and me. (Again, this situation had its pros and cons and maintaining a sense of humor helped.)

Because my move was to a new state I was put on a waiting list to get services. My Mom worked hard to get acquainted with the area—always looking for ways that I could connect with people in the community and participate in activities in some way. On Friday nights during the summertime the city would have bands play and people would gather to listen and dance. Both Grandma and I loved music so this was something everyone could enjoy. As Grandma got older she needed to use a wheelchair like me. This is the good thing about needing a wheelchair to get around—you automatically come with your own seating! The rest of my family had to bring lawn chairs. It was no simple task to load us all up for the short drive to downtown and then unload everything while monitoring that Grandma and I are safe from rolling away. (There are lots of little hills where we live now.) Eventually we would all be situated to listen to the music for a couple hours.

Grandma didn't like being dependent on other people. Sometimes she would want to help and try to do stuff on her own that would put her at risk for hurting herself. But sometimes she would find other ways to contribute that were really helpful. For example, she would often offer to feed me lunch or dinner.

Let me explain before I go on: I cannot eat by myself. Because I am legally blind and don't have the greatest fine motor skills it is hard for me to use spoons and forks. It is even hard for me to eat things like soup because I cannot close my mouth with the same skill as most people.

Most people do not appreciate how magnificent the human body is. There are so many things we learn to do that do not need to be taught. The mind and body work together to learn how to accomplish certain tasks like eating. My mom had to teach me how to chew. I will always have trouble with eating things like stew because I do not have the kind of control and coordination required of my tongue and mouth—not to mention the coordination required to bring the spoon to my mouth without spilling.

My mom has taught me to bring a filled spoon (filled with something that won't easily fall off) to my mouth. And just this last year I have learned to return the spoon to the bowl. (My mom found these great bowls that work well for me. You see, it is very complicated. Remember I can't see and I am likely to bump things which may result in my spilling or dropping something which will upset me....and there we go...If I mess things up enough that I begin to focus on the fact that I am still hungry I'll get even more angry with myself. Fortunately, this doesn't happen often. This is why my mom always does her best to set up my environment for success.

My Aunt Chris is both amazed that I do manage to usually get the spoon to my mouth without spilling and annoyed that I have to take the long route to my mouth—first extending my hand with filled spoon out to my side a bit, while bouncing my arm up and down a bit, while pounding lightly on the table with my other hand, all while making gurgling sounds. She has learned to trust that everything will be okay. It is just another life lesson learned in the nitty-gritty of getting me through a day. Everything will be okay. Now, instead of worrying she watches with a touch of amusement as I demonstrate my skill at providing her opportunities to learn that.

Although filled with potential messes my independence is worth it. It would be too tricky for Grandma to help me feed myself so Grandma fed me at times when I needed more help.

Grandma would often sing to me when we were waiting for breakfast to be done cooking. There was one song on my keyboard that she especially liked. I would press the song button until that song came up and I would listen while Grandma sang the song. I loved to listen to her sing along so I would play that song over and over again until she would get tired and ask me to please play another song. Grandma passed away a couple of years ago and I quit playing that song for the most part. But, every once in a while when I play that song everyone says, "There's Grandma's song!" and remembers those times Grandma helped me. I don't usually listen to the whole song like I used to when Grandma sang along. I have one particular song in the rotation of songs that I go to over and over again. No one knows why I like this song but they are amazed that I can determine that I am at that song before even the second note is played. I say "wonder" when I get there. I don't hesitate to celebrate my successes!

I think everyone should celebrate their successes. I enjoy it when people around me are laughing or singing. Although often I will seem to be in my own little world not paying attention to what is going on around me, if people are laughing I may well make a point of joining in. My mom thinks that sometimes I may figure that people are laughing because I did something cute. I say, again, nothing wrong with celebrating me. As a matter of fact no matter what people may have been laughing about after my mom says this then everyone shifts their focus to me and laughs along with me. Guess I'm right no matter how you look at it!

We had quite a full house when we first moved to our new house. I enjoyed having so much family around each day. (It wasn't until after Grandma died that the lower level was finished so Mom and

I could have our own space designed especially to meet my needs.) Still, Mom, as usual, wanted to get me out into the community like I was when I lived in the other states. Besides listening to the bands those summer nights Mom got me exerwheeling at the malls again. We tried a mall close to home but it had carpet that was hard for me to wheel on, and the lighting was bad, and there weren't many stores open which means not a lot of people. For a few years I went to a mall that was forty-five minutes away. I made some connections there and worked on saying hi again. I even got massages there. That was wonderful! But, just a few months ago Mom figured out that with the price of gas being so high it would make more sense to get a membership at a fitness center ten minutes from home. And, I could go a lot more often. Plus, I would be exerwheeling with walkers from my very own community. Plus, plus, plus, I can get my massage there weekly. That helps my body relax—and my mind.

I am also able to attend a Zumba class there one or two days a week. The class is small so I am welcome to join in like I used to in line dancing. At this point I just enjoy the music. Someone noticed once that I danced along (bopped my hand up and down to the music) but just for a brief second. Mom hopes that eventually I will "dance" even more to the music. She and my personal trainer (as a member I get some free sessions each year!) are looking at ways I can participate in other areas—like the pool. My personal trainer is very excited about the pool and she is always trying to think of thinks I may be able to do. She has a lot of energy and is always happy to see me.

Another one of the trainers who has worked with my Mom also says hi. A lot of the walkers say hi too. My mom has been a member there for a while and a lot of folks know I am her son. I enjoy going there. I feel welcome. There is one lady who makes a point of saying, "I am glad you are here!" each time I see her. It is nice to hear. I think maybe everyone should make a point of saying this to others when that is what they feel. Too often we don't even notice the joy we feel when we run into a friend. It really feels good to hear it, so when you feel it, say it. That's my advice anyway.

Until just recently, before my mom put me on a gluten free diet like she is on, I seemed to have lost some of my skills for a number of years. It seemed my vision had gotten even worse. I quit watching the TV when cartoons were on. I quit pointing so much to get people to tell me what things are. I quit using some of the phrases and words I used to use. I didn't wheel around the house like I used to (although learning a new environment can be tricky). I quit using my right hand while exerwheeling.

No one knows if it was the dietary change that made the difference or something else. But I now really watch cartoons—even more than I used to. And I am wheeling myself around more and more at home which helps me better communicate what I would like to do. I again am getting my supports to label things for me when I point and ask, "Whaz a?" And, I am starting to use my right hand when exerwheeling again. I also enjoy seeing myself in the mirror again. When asked, "Who's in there?" or "Who's that handsome guy?" (a favorite of mine), I am getting better and better at saying "Co-y". My latest thing is wanting to have the table cleared of what I see as unnecessary stuff. Mom and I are in the process of negotiating on that. You see there are always pros and cons to my increased participation in controlling my life! You have to keep a sense of humor about these things.

Throughout the years I have kept my mom guessing about what is going on with me, whether it is my behavior or my health. I am not able to communicate what is going on with me so she has to figure things out without my help. She has learned how to read little signals I make when something is wrong. Everyone in the house knows when a storm is coming because I'll start pounding my ears and making noise even though they can't hear the thunder yet. But, that is an easy one. What is going on with me can be a lot more complicated.

I have gone through periods of refusing to eat or having difficulty eating since I was a little kid. At one point I even had a tube in my stomach. The only way to figure out what is going on with me is to watch me closely and come up with an idea of what might be happening and then trying something different to see if it works. Often it is hard to tell whether whatever I was going through was temporary, or something I was able to work through myself, or whether some change she made is what made the difference. Mom and Aunt Chris will often bounce ideas off one another. In the end there are probably more times than not that they feel they really don't know what was going on. Fortunately, overall things work out well because I am mostly happy and Mom and Aunt Chris do know this for sure.

Rules to Live By

By Cory Seiler

- Take time to notice and appreciate the small things:
    - being outside
    - feeling the warmth of the sun
    - feeling the freshness of the breeze
    - the sounds of motorcycles, planes, roosters
    - long relaxing rides
    - christmas lights
    - christmas songs
    - riding elevators
    - lights and shadows
    - your own reflection in the mirror
- Live life in the present moment, don't worry about the past or fear what's going to happen tomorrow.
- Keep a sense of humor about things.
- Everything will be okay.

- Celebrate your successes.
- Wonder about the possibilities!

If you want to teach me something:

- Pay very close attention to me—the things I do, the reactions I have. You will learn a lot.
- Know that if I am not motivated to do something, it's not likely that I'll learn how to do it. (Would you?)
- Know that participating in everyday activities as much as I can makes me feel good. I love to make things happen. (Don't you?)
- Set my environment up for success.
- Know that independence is worth what it takes.
- Routine helps me predict what will be happening to me; but also, allow me to experience new and exotic things.
- Remember people with disabilities are both "regular" and "special". (As are you!)

What I have learned about relating to others:

- Let people know you appreciate what they do for you.
- A smile or a little laughter goes a long way.
- It is important to make people feel good.
- When you are happy to see someone let them know.
- Take connecting with others in stride: Always give people the opportunity to come through. Be glad if they do and figure they weren't ready if they don't. Be prepared to give them another opportunity.
- People are usually great when given the opportunity to be so.

About the Author

Christine Seiler began working with children with disabilities as a high school volunteer at the University of Minnesota's summer program for learners with autism. Still in her teens, she became "Aunt Chris" to Cory, who is profoundly affected by multiple disabilities including autism. As doors opened in her college days, she became interested in working with senior high students with emotional/behavioral issues. She worked as a teacher with them for a number of years before leaving the security of her home and job, venturing out to see what the universe had in store for her next.

Because of her role as Cory's aunt, she always maintained an interest in parent and family advocacy. In completing her doctoral studies in special education at the University of South Florida, her dissertation, *Making Meaning of their Role as Advocates: Parents of Children with Developmental Disabilities,* gave voice to parents of children with developmental disabilities.

Christine has come to recognize that the children with disabilities that she has known in her life have been her spiritual teachers. All she needed to do was be open to what they had to teach.

Christine, who now lives in North Carolina, continues to believe that there is a lot of power in personal stories. She continues to encourage people to tell their stories in ways that empower both themselves and others.